THICKET

AUCKLAND UNIVERSITY PRESS

Poems from *Thicket* have been published, sometimes in slightly different forms, in the following publications: *Best New Zealand Poems, Blackmail Press, Broadsheet, Cordite, Heat, International Literary Quarterly, New Zealand Listener, Landfall, The Manchester Review, Moving Worlds, The Page, PNReview, Snorkel, Trout, Turbine* and in a Festschrift for Vincent O'Sullivan, *Still Shines When You Think Of It*.

First published 2011

Auckland University Press
University of Auckland
Private Bag 92019
Auckland 1142, New Zealand
www.auckland.ac.nz/aup

© Anna Jackson, 2011

ISBN 978 1 86940 482 6

Publication is kindly assisted by

National Library of New Zealand Cataloguing-in-Publication Data
Jackson, Anna, 1967-
Thicket / Anna Jackson.
ISBN 978-1-86940-482-6
I. Title.
NZ821.2—dc 22

This book is copyright. Apart from fair dealing for the purpose of private study, research, criticism or review, as permitted under the Copyright Act, no part may be reproduced by any process without prior permission of the publisher.

Cover design: Athena Sommerfeld
Cover image: Kathryn Madill, *The Red Forest – Rat-A-Tat-Tat* (detail), 2010.
Photograph by Bill Nichol

Printed by Ligare Ltd, Auckland

CONTENTS

Watch this	1
Marry in haste	2
Basement	3
Badminton	4
Virgil at bedtime	6
Dream golems	7
Speaking as one of the billiard balls	8
Ophthalmoscope	9
Red Riding Hood's mother	10
Red Riding Hood	11
Second puppet	12
Spring	13
It was an honour, John	14
Margo, or Margaux	15
Frank O'Hara for Charles	17
Unknown unknowns	19
We were at the British Museum?	21
The coming on of a maths brain	23
A beautiful theory isn't a poem, James	26
For some reason	28

It's just glass	29
Giving up	31
Doubling back	33
Wondering how to see it	34
Envelope	35
Indexing	36
Ghostess	37
Zina at the zoo	38
Seeing you	40
Stand too close	41
Imogen	42
The fish and I	43
Salty hair	44
Not looking, feeling	45
Poetry, and its returns	47
Hansel in the house	48
Exit, pursued	49
Let alone	50
My brother, twelve swans	51
Autumn	52
Summer	53
Notes	54

WATCH THIS

Time to get real.
You're getting older –

you should think about getting
a tiny house strapped to your arm,

with a tiny mortgage to pay.
And when a tiny child runs out,

you should strap that child
around your arm till it grows up –

here is your watch,
you can say to it then.

MARRY IN HASTE

Pull down the white curtain –
nothing you already have will do.

Cut a little distance from the outline of yourself,
you have to have room to breathe. Then sew.

Stitch by stitch it should come together.
It doesn't matter about the weather,

you don't get married to feel warm, or cold.
It turns out you can repent at pressure,

from when you are young,
till when you grow old.

BASEMENT

The gutted basement is what
we *like* about the house.
We can live perfectly well
upstairs, over our dreams
of those new interlocking
floorboards, eight centimetres
thick, that we'll have laid
downstairs. Sliding
doors, walls we imagine
in different places,
it is all we talk about
for months, while
we leave the gas leaking
upstairs again, forgetting
to light the flames.
I quite *like* the smell.
We'll put the children
downstairs, when it's built.
And build a basement
under them, more gutted
floors, broken concrete
and disconnected sinks,
somewhere to move
the junk down to,
and plan to floor as well.

BADMINTON

It's not a dumb *game*, you're dumb
at it. Though it doesn't help
to say that, and you're getting
better. This is probably
the only day we'll ever get
to play like this, you realise,
it won't work in the wind, and
this is *Wellington*. We
don't have a net, we're just
counting volleys, pretty
good to hit three, then
we hit five, then our world
record of seven.
We're going for eight,
even if the clothesline
gets in the way, even if
that lunge back has me falling
backwards over the wall
that came down in the storm,
into the compost, trying to get up
in time for your next shot,
stepping further back
down the bank, stumbling
over the blackberry vine,
feeling for the concrete steps
buried somewhere under the grass,
because we've got to beat

eleven now, and although
it is getting dark, there is still
the thwack of *something*
on the strings I've hit,
and I can hear someone
stumbling down the bank
after me, hitting
something, and who
could it *be* except
for you?

VIRGIL AT BEDTIME

There are glow-in-the-dark stars
on the ceiling which probably
won't peel off. And yes, there are
two gates of sleep, sweet heart,
it is not just in the morning
you have to be careful what side
of the bed you choose,
there are choices to make
day and night,
and for the rest of your life.
And the ivory gate *is* glittering
but not smiling at you,
it is just the way it is shaped
like the mouth of a crocodile
opening wide,
offering futures like vistas,
dreams that will
eat you up.
No, the other gate is the gate
to choose, sweet heart,
and your dreams, if you dream,
will be safe as houses
and won't bankrupt you at all –
you just have to be dead
to go through.

DREAM GOLEMS

It can't just be me whose thoughts
outgrow reality sometimes,
but won't be expelled from my head
like a placenta to be buried
under a tree (which the children think
is gross, anyway – they suggest
liquefying the placenta
so you can flush it out
as food for fish).
What *do* you do with dreams
you've got no use for?
If truth is spelt *emet,* you
can scratch off the *e* and be left
with *met,* spelling death
and the end of it –
but my golems are Pakeha
golems, spelt in English,
and when I scratch off the *t* from
truth, I'm left with *ruth.*
And the more I rue my dreams
the more they talk back to me,
they feed on my ruth
to grow realer than me,
they haunt my life as the ghost
I can't give up till I die –
and when I say *they,*
I mean one at a time,
in a kind of dream monogamy.

SPEAKING AS ONE OF THE BILLIARD BALLS

The film *Troy* doesn't start till after dark,
four hours after school's out. So I take
Johnny up to the pool hall where
I have to teach him *not* to take turns –
except that neither of us pot a ball
very much more often than rolling a six
in Snakes and Ladders.
It isn't easy, working always
with ricochet – later, we'll watch
Troy, and see the gods
misjudge. Speaking
as one of the balls, when
those divine passions hit me next
I'm going to try and remember
that 1) even if I hit the right target
it still probably won't have the intended effect
and 2) in any case, the effect that is intended
isn't the effect that the impact
is going to have on me.

OPHTHALMOSCOPE

Technically, it is the light
of the ophthalmoscope
throwing my veins out
in front of my vision
knotting themselves
into a forest
between us.
Or surrounding us,
it seems like, that
knocking sound
unlikely to be a gardener
arriving at last
to clear things out,
or a midwife at the door
to perform any kind
of delivery,
and we can't expect
a *postal* delivery
in this situation,
or, obviously, a guest.
It could be a joke.
Who's there?
We'll have stepped back
before the punchline,
the second name.
One week, you promise,
before I'll see clearly again.

RED RIDING HOOD'S MOTHER

I am the angel in the house,
looking for the keys.

Can you answer the phone,
and don't talk to me like that.

I gave birth to two children
from my animal womb

and they eat up all my food
and mess up all the rooms.

I am looking for the keys
in the eyes of the storm,

in the storm of my son,
in the dawn of my daughter,

in the ought to of the would.
I am the angel in the wood.

RED RIDING HOOD

She is always looking back to before me.
Me, she sends outside, while she searches

in cupboards and books.
I'm sent into the woods.

I'll go back too.
I'll ask her mother what she was like as a child.

How did you get through the woods
so fast, Grandmother asks me instead.

Not like your mother.
Always so wild.

SECOND PUPPET

I will be the second puppet,
smiling at the puppet laughing.

My eyes will be open
but sly.

I will be the puppet with eyebrows
raised high.

The reason my shirt is more crumpled
is I am the one you touch.

It is my choice to be second puppet,
and not to laugh so much.

SPRING

All day today the ice melted.
My name is Queen.
I haven't melted at all
though I am soft
and getting softer
until I will pardon you all.
I watch benignly as one by one
you slink off down diminishing avenues
to somewhere less central.
I pardon Jimmy who egged on Joe
who threw the snowball at Jean
and I pardon Jean for wiping off the snow
as if snow were something that should go.
Even the grass is pushing snow aside.
I can feel it rising up inside me, too.
I pardon it
and get on with my reign.

IT WAS AN HONOUR, JOHN

I have spent the morning preparing and when he arrives,
my heart in my mouth, the linen on the table,

it all looks like a picture, a magazine spread.
We uncork the wine, break the bread, everything still

to be said, jokes at first, anecdotes, gossip about writers
he knows and I have read, then the complaints

and consolations, between interruptions from the children,
and by the third bottle of wine, recriminations, accusations,

unforgivable remarks. Till it is dark, and unsteadily
he makes a move to depart. Instead, we walk

the alcohol off by the light of the moon, passing
the baby when our arms tire, quiet now, except to remark

on the extraordinary lucidity of the sky, the clouds,
so diffuse by daylight, by night so strangely defined.

MARGO, OR MARGAUX

I'd drink all night but stop at one glass
of syrah, aromas of pepper, tar,
black plum, and on the tongue
blueberry, liquorice, dark
chocolate, oh it is a dark wine
for us to drink before entering
the night in my cream and silver
car and driving, *reeling*,
not from the wine but from
the gypsy pirate Mexican music
on the CD (with an after-note, you
suggest, of Ukrainian folk), under
your canopy of silver stars.
Don't tell me their names, tracing
out constellations like
a dot-to-dot puzzle. Let me
see the *sky* in the sky, as magisterially
as the sea can be seen in the sea
and the man in the man – speaking
of which let's *not* meet your mother
with her photos of you as a boy.
Let's just keep driving to
somewhere we haven't looked up
on a map, some town without
any relatives to pin your features
down to theirs, where you can do
that silent thing you do at parties

in a party we'll throw
just for us two.
This cross made up of freckles
under my ribs (two brown, one
red and slightly raised, one beige)
might *look* like the Southern Cross
still flying like a kite in the chaos
I've relearned to see in the sky,
but come closer, inhale,
tell me my after-notes
and under-tones,
and whether you think
I should call my car Margo or
Margaux, I can't decide.

FRANK O'HARA FOR CHARLES

So it is 10.03 (this is when I still had my watch on)
and Charles and I are on our way through the rain
to Bill's Frank O'Hara lecture and Charles says
but anyone could write a Frank O'Hara poem, why
bother? And he sits through the lecture
in his black leather jacket, his trainers
up on the metal ring bit of his chair,
his arms folded against his linen shirt,
and when I accidentally yell 'goody' when Bill
says he'll play Frank O'Hara's recording
of 'Song' he says 'try and be a *bit*
more academic, Anna.' Then Frank O'Hara
in a sweet and Ginsberg-like voice is repeating
his refrain, 'you don't refuse to breathe
do you,' and I am thinking, if anyone
can write a Frank O'Hara poem, isn't that
a *good* thing? Doesn't that make us all
potentially good people? As if Ginsberg
had got it right and 'we're all golden
sunflowers inside,' as I try and tell Charles
who tells me to pipe down and listen
to the lecture, and I have to admit that later, in our
tutorial class, after listening to Ginsberg
giving a most elegiac and O'Hara-like rendition
of 'America' on the computer with Windows
Media Player, when we start looking at Plath,
she does seem to keep her inner sunflower

pretty much hidden although I try
and make a case for reading the poems
as a literary exercise and the suicide
as an accident and Frank O'Hara poetry
as what she could have been writing
if she weren't so determined
to think up something new and different
to do to interest the critics. I still think
she could have. Anyone could! So let's!
Who knows what it might save us from?
After all, anyone can talk,
and you don't refuse to talk, do you?

UNKNOWN UNKNOWNS

Maybe one day we will even teach in schools,
along with Homer again, and the *Aeneid*,
the equally complex songs of the whale,
graduate students composing theories
about the mysterious bass shift
in song latitude 61° longitude 15°
towards the end of 1971 –
still, we will never know the secret song
the whale sings to himself,
the heretic variations,
the secret pleasure
he allows himself
in the silence and the dark;
any more than the poet's biographer,
revealing everything he's told,
accounting for contradictions
in accounts, gaps in the paper trail,
can know where the poet goes at night
when even his wife, lying beside him
in the dark, can't know where he goes
in the privacy of his mind;
any more than we can know
what other worlds God might have dreamed up
too secret, too sentimental,
too erotic to be manifest
in the universe
of dust and light;

any more than we can know
it isn't this one after all
that is the imaginary world
too sentimental, too beautiful,
too privately pleasurable
really to be real.

WE WERE AT THE BRITISH MUSEUM?

There is the smallest grain of something on the sheet
I have to keep moving away from only to meet
again somewhere else in this hotel room bed
and when I finally shift myself clear
there is a shiver in my ear
and my feet itch,
and my scalp,
as if there is something walking
from hair to hair.
Or is it my skin crawling?
And is it just going to crawl
around and around the edges of me
or is it going to crawl free
leaving me
to wake in the morning
unravelled, the bits of me that have travelled
not even me? And
if all night I have seen
what they see, calling this dreaming
would be like failing to see the holes between
the atoms and calling it beauty.
Oh, but that really is beautiful.
We were at the British Museum?
And the explanation offered
in the Egyptian room
kept dividing into three:
body, heart, spirit is just the start,

then spirit into *ka*, *ba* and *akh*,
ka, the spiritual double of the body
pictured as a pair of arms,
ba, the spirit that travels, from
the body, in the night
and on beyond the life,
and *akh*, the spirit that aspires to be immortal,
the possibility
open as the holes between atoms
that *human* might be *god* . . .
In the meantime, the resin and wrappings
for the body, entrapping
the itchy *ba*.
There was a mummified *fish*!
For the mummified cats?
Or to allow for fish *ba*
to flow to and from fish body,
merrily merrily merrily
without itch or seam?

THE COMING ON OF A MATHS BRAIN

The
world
unfurled
unfurling
all over again –
for a real mathematician
a walk round the block must be a symphony swirling,

all
those
perfect
ratios.
Though also I guess
there must be ratios that clash –
where I see the green lawn clashing with the blue windows,

he
sees
what would
be good squares
of window and lawn
ruined by the wrong proportion
of the (I think) beautifully cream-coloured front door.

And
what
of all
the other

senses, touch and smell
and taste and hearing? My *brother*
could tell you music is maths, *obviously* the fall

from
note
to note
and the count
of skipped sound amounts
to what music is all about,
but are there (for example) mathematical chefs out

there,
who
tell you
star anise
(being twenty-one)
can sit next to ginger (thirteen)
but in a mixture with saffron (six) could never please,

the
maths
does not
allow it?
No wonder I get
cooking so wrong, no math brain yet
developed in me, though like late-growing wisdom teeth

my
maths
brain may
I think be
coming on, today
perhaps the day its growth begins . . .
Tonight when we curl up in bed, I'll measure our match.*

* If we don't fit the golden mean I'll unwrite these lines,
reverse the poem's onward growth,
hold on to the both
of us as
the maths
that
counts.

A BEAUTIFUL THEORY ISN'T A POEM, JAMES

I still haven't written a duck poem although
the duck was good, what can I say, was *so*

good, but now it is more like three *weeks* later
that I am once again leaving an elevator

with James, and I have a theory I want to unfold
to him about tequila and wine: how wine will hold

the moment open in all its ripeness and let you sit
in the present tense for an evening, but *tequila*, it

is like a terrible vortex drink, that tries to pull
all the future and all the past into the swill

of the moment you drink it in, and there you are
trying to relive some other night at another bar

on someone else's lap and James is referring to that
conversation you've never even had with him yet

about Diana's apples and the next morning, your
hangover is not at all the melancholy despair

for the future and regret for the past that wine
induces, but an unrelenting present tense return

to precisely the moment you were trying to swill
yourself out of, a moment all the worse for being full

of you, and what you did. So. I get out of the elevator
three days after the tequila night, reborn as a stater

of tequila theory, and now James is waiting for me
to put it all into a poem. But a beautiful theory

isn't a poem, James. A beautiful theory is only
a theory.

FOR SOME REASON

This was when all the people
I was painting had vegetable
bodies – carrots and turnips,
root vegetables. Even I
started wondering
what I meant
by them, especially
the postcard versions
I was sending out to friends.
Not being able to draw
bodies very well,
getting stuck
trying to make the hands
and legs look right,
isn't *interpretation*.
And when I wonder
what it is that God
can't draw
to have to make *our*
capacities to manipulate
and also to escape
so stunted,
well, what sort
of a turnip is *that*
for a thought, what
can't I really think
to have to end up so
theological all the time?

IT'S JUST GLASS

If the theologians no longer believe
in the physical resurrection
of Christ, am *I* going to have to
start to? If it's all metaphor
now, might as *well* give
it over to poets,
it's as pallid as poetry this
separation of the historical reality
from anything it might mean
later, but if it's really all up
for grabs I'm believing
in the Greek gods. *Narrative*
gods I'm looking for,
who'll take an interest
in a good story and give
the narrative potential of my life
a push, if I can get them
to notice me –
what will my colleague say
when I suggest we mark
only the Gatsby answers
this year? *You mark
as Daisy, I'll mark
as Wilson.* Don't ask
is that hole in the windscreen
real or metaphorical –
it's just glass,
we don't need it,

wrap a tea-towel round your hand
and knock it out.
Do it or less,
the gods ought to shout.

GIVING UP

It *is* the room I want, room
to deny myself, the spaciousness
of humility, not the empty air
of the scrambling vines
but the rich earth
where the potato digs down.
There in the dark there is all the room
you need to go nowhere at all.
No, I couldn't believe harder
in scrambling after nothing
at all but staying still, if only
the scrambling upwards
wasn't so much *fun*,
putting out the leaves, feeling
for the next hold
to haul the whole self
upwards with –
what a lark!
The potato has eyes
but the sprout isn't shouting
look at me,
just heading up
for the – for *headiness* is all.
I'm giving up humility.
I'll throw it away
to be a scrambling vine.
For sure, at the end

of it all, the potato
will be saved,
the vine returned
to the earth –
well, I'll have my room then,
I'll *welcome* the worms in.

DOUBLING BACK

I've taken to writing every shopping list
twice, once in the order I use things up
and once in the order of the aisles,
but still I'm always doubling back,
leaving my trolley
by the frozen foods,
and then forgetting
to remember ice.
Every year seems shorter than the year before –
yet when I work out the cost of things
in terms of time, everything gets cheaper
as if the years were getting longer
by the minute.
I'll just have to put more *in* to it,
fill up with abstractions
that can travel so vastly
every year will be like an ocean liner
with a swimming pool on the top floor,
the length of the swim
depending entirely on how often
you want to swim back, and forth.

WONDERING HOW TO SEE IT

You can't say I didn't throw myself in,
ready (drunk) to be rushed off
in a current, over whatever
there was to fall down,
and here I am – still
drunk, finding the water
warm, slightly saline,
after all this time
beginning to *congeal*,
feeling in some places
almost solid, forming a *skin*
within the pool. A membrane
to hatch through? Or a *contact lens,*
for an eye a whole lot bigger than my life?

ENVELOPE

I stick a stamp on an envelope.
It is a lake, a little glassy, and a mountain, behind the lake.
A little bit of lake is left behind on my tongue.

I would not like to be a fish in that lake.
A little bit of me would always be going missing.
I would always be leaving the lake for the mountain.

And now, it is several days later.
I am waiting for a reply.
Then I see that the stamp is still attached to me.

So that explains my demonic energy lately!
That explains how I rose so high so fast,
what everyone means when they refer to my depth.

But where am I being sent?
And when I arrive, who will open me?
Roughly, with a finger, or gently, with a knife?

INDEXING

And then it is all over, and we leave life behind
like a daytime movie, emerging dazzled –

it is so much clearer now, so much brighter!
(Not so much story, of course, but still.)

All over! Except for the indexing:
and though no one believes judgement depends on it,

still we labour to do it right.
You index achievements, I index my dreams –

> bears, 3.4.1971, 21:19; 6.4.1971, 23.45; 11.10.1971,
> 21.38–44; 1.1.1972, 01:22 etc.
> birds, 7.4.1971, 21:48–49; 13.5.1973, 23:40; 6.10.1982,
> 22:10; 12.6.1984, 22:11; 14.10.1995, 02:40; and
> brothers, 12.12.1990, 06:40; 11.05.2010, 03:13

But perhaps it is our appearances
in others' indexes that count.

Well, I am in your index,
and you are in mine.

GHOSTESS

I was not around in those Gay Edwardian days
when young aristocrats and men of fashion
came to London to indulge their pleasures.
I did not attend, as a guest or ghost,
any of the legendary dinners
cooked by the fabulous Mrs Rosa Lewis,
I did not wear an evening gown
and have my hair done London style.
I did not, raising my champagne glass
to smash it dangerously hard
against the glass of the man across
from me, suddenly feel
the world double and split
with a sensation of *déjà vu,*
as if I saw myself or had already been seen
by some future ghost of myself whom
I could never come to have been,
I did not look across and see
in the glass windows
of the glittering St James Hotel
reflected the pinched
and haunted face,
the frown between the brows,
of anyone watching me.

ZINA AT THE ZOO

After all, I have to do something with myself.
Walking around and around isn't any more tiring

than trying to sleep, at night, and thinking of you.
And after you, there will be someone else,

this is only the intermission,
I am, after all, Russian.

I will not look back like Lot's wife looked back
till I might as well be made of salt,

I will not cry a single tear for you,
leave it to the men

to send elaborate telegrams in the night
after it is all over,

to declare that if there are stars in the sky,
they must be there because without them some lovesick poet
  would die.

I'll walk my little dog at the zoo.
I read once that a lion can love a little dog –

he might tear the first five or so to pieces
but he'll love the sixth . . .

I'd be torn to pieces five times
to be loved by a lion.

I must be nearly up to my sixth . . .
Oh I can't *tell* you the extent to which I'm over you.

SEEING YOU

Seeing you makes me nearly crash
into so many people, including

the girl whose hair piled up
on her head and deliberately fake

application of rouge on her cheeks,
also the dangling ear-rings,

you'd think would give her
an exhibitionist air,

yet perhaps she is trying to distract
from her beauty, not flaunt it,

or at least not flaunt it at me, whose
surreptitious observation of her

for the last couple of blocks
I think she must have noticed,

from the way, when I nearly crash
into her now, she flinches

in the manner of someone feeling
they are being nearly crashed into

on purpose, whereas, really,
it was just the surprise of seeing you!

STAND TOO CLOSE

Take it from my waist
and tie it around your neck,
like a ribbon around a tree.
Now do you remember me?
Then tie it around my waist – loosely,
as if I were bigger
than me.
If this were a room
in a *Vogue* magazine,
it would hang loosely over a chair,
as if I had just come in
and then walked out again.
If this were a room
in a Vermeer
it would only be here
if someone was wearing it
or if someone was tying it, or if
someone was using it to scrub the floor
down on their hands and knees.
Not me.
Stand too close
and I will look past your ear
till the background noise recedes,
and only the rest is here.

IMOGEN

Innocence built her open
inside,

anger,
a glorious spray,

hunger,
a shore that love rode in to.

We were all watching
Imogen.

Even you had to admit
he was good for her,

the calm coming to seem
like home.

THE FISH AND I

I wasn't really fishing,
just walking by the sea,
liking the way the gulls rise
up in front of me,
not expecting a fish to jump out at me.
And all I did was throw it back.
I wasn't going to carry it home,
it is always a long walk home from the sea,
though never as far as it was then.
It was a long time before I realised I had arrived.
It wasn't the home I had left behind.
It wasn't anything I'd asked for.
But you can't throw a marriage,
children, a job, back
into the sea . . .
Oh, when did I ever, *ever*,
ask for anything?
Except, always, not to have
mortified myself in all the ways
I mortify myself every day . . .
I'm not afraid of the ditch at the end of it all.
I just wish it could end like it does
in the story, and I could go back
to nothing while I still got
to be alive, have
a turn at being
the *fish* for a change.

SALTY HAIR

In the morning my pillow is wet through
to the sheets. I have to wring out
the salt from my hair before
I can lift my head
and drink five cups of coffee
before I can speak – but when I open
my mouth an ocean pours out
from my eyes. I know
just how glaciers must feel
when spring comes on, loosening
from the inside out, leaking all
those hard-won centimetres
out in a rush to the sea,
and the *sea*, oh I know how
the *sea* feels, swallowing more and more
with more still coming at it, not a hope
of lying still when you are overflowing, your
own insides turning endlessly over
and beaching themselves on each
and every shore.
You wish the *shores* would go away.
But thank you, all the same,
for holding out your sands.

NOT LOOKING, FEELING

I know not to look at the faces
lined up to judge, just dance
as best as I can, aim for the point
I must reach across the room,
focus on the landing of my feet,
complicated by the need to avoid
the bits of Lego and plastic cars
still covering the floor –
unbelievable that I did not tidy first.
But don't think about it, only
the rhythm and the next step
in the sequence, turning
the skittering into a slide,
the twinge of pain into the impetus
for the most forceful turn
I've ever given this part of the dance,
making it the emotional hinge
of the whole affair . . .
I can't look up at the faces
when I stop moving
but keep moving,
not dancing now but picking up
the bits of plastic, searching for the Lego bin
and the lid to wedge on top of it,
fitting a sock into a teapot,
shoving the teapot down
into the collapsible toy basket,

past the soft giraffe that came free
with the cough medicine, past
the bear with the wobbling eye,
down past everything soft
and forgotten to the very bottom
where I hit the dust and paper scraps
and where I grasp a dream, or a dream
grasps me, entering my fingertips
like sap, rising beyond my wrist
and up my arm, and on beyond
the elbow and above, until
my whole body turns to wood
and I stand here as a tree,
am standing still . . .
these pages
my leaves that talk for me.

POETRY, AND ITS RETURNS

The poem prints out terribly shadowy.
You'll have to take it to someone higher up.

Only, the lift doesn't come
no matter how hard you press the call button.

Beauty and a question –
or a question mark –

that's all anyone can make out.
Poetry is no urn to catch things in.

Throw it –
the animal that brings it back

is all that was ever truly yours.
Wait for it, it is coming up the stairs.

HANSEL IN THE HOUSE

When you lie in your bed at night
hearing your parents talking?

That's the sound of your coffin
being assembled for you to climb in.

That's when you have to get out
of the house, of their life.

And all you want from them
is to leave the door open.

All you want . . .

All you want is for them
never to wish you were gone.

EXIT, PURSUED

The weekend, and the same direction
over and over, *exit, pursued*
by my son.
Anything to avoid a row.
I suppose I do become a little wooden
and to my son, exiled
in his own *Aeneid*,
might look a little less like Love
than I did once.
It does feel, pursued by my son,
as if he doesn't know whom he pursues,
or what he's asking for
except to tell this stranger
how strange a world it is for him,
how hard his exile,
how unprovisioned,
how inadequate
so wooden a response.

LET ALONE

Stumbling into the dark, feeling
for the concrete steps buried
somewhere under the grass,
stepping over the blackberry vines,
how can I even stop to see
who is pursuing me,
let alone make out
the changes imposed
on you by this exile,
these hardships
you recount,
let *alone* stop long enough
to spin anything I could fling over you
to make you into a man.
It will have to be the sister you fly from
as it is in the stories,
after years of her
hardly saying a word.

MY BROTHER, TWELVE SWANS

It is always my mother who drives him wild
until, finally, he takes flight –

and I am left silent in the house.
I won't be driven wild by my mother.

I hold my tongue, bide my time,
carry her basket into the wood.

I'd walk up *glass* to reach my brother.
Twelve times I throw my spinning over him,

twelve times watch him turn from beast to man.
What do I even want him for?

To reduce him to nothing like myself?
And still I stop short
               of the final wing . . .

AUTUMN

The top of her hair still dry
and her mouth half in half out of the water –

you are growing taller, I announce,
towelling my daughter.

I wonder if she remembers
pastel storm clouds overhead

and someone shouting,
someone reaching out.

SUMMER

These are our thicket days
and it does seem darker,

though the sun is at its peak
over the crown of leaves.

Having climbed at last to the tasket dais
we demand better titles

to make up for the weight we carry,
and all we have achieved.

This is a thicket,
not a casket,
and one day we'll walk out;

ears ringing,
flask empty,
a drought in the mouth.

NOTES

'Virgil at bedtime'
From Virgil, *The Aeneid*, translated by Robert Fitzgerald (Harvill Press), chapter six, lines 892–896: 'There are two gates of Sleep, one said to be / Of horn, whereby the true shades pass with ease, / The other all white ivory agleam / Without a flaw, and yet false dreams are sent / Through this one by the ghosts of the upper world.'

'The coming on of a maths brain'
This is a 'fib', a poetic form invented by Gregory K. Pincus, using the Fibonacci sequence to determine the syllable length of each line. For Pincus's instructions on writing 'fibbery', go to http://gottabook.blogspot.com/2006/04/more-fibbery.html

'Giving up'
A 1901 school story, *Tom and Some Other Girls*, concludes with the heroine, Rhoda, understanding that what she needs is not, as she thought school would give her, 'room to distinguish herself', but rather 'room to deny herself'. It makes such a striking contrast with Virginia Woolf's conclusion a generation later that what a woman needs is 'a room of one's own' that I wanted to give the idea some room in this poem.

'Zina at the zoo'
The starting point for this poem was Sasha Cherny's short story 'Micky the Fox Terrier's Diary' which I originally used as the basis for a poem, 'Micky the fox terrier at the zoo'. Zina appears in Cherny's story from Micky's point of view.

'The fish and I'
This is a retelling of the old folk tale about the fisherman who is persuaded to release a fish back into the sea in exchange for a wish. His wish for a house to live in initially delights his wife but eventually she becomes dissatisfied with their cottage and sends him back to ask the fish for a larger house. As her aspirations continue to rise, the fish is pulled out of the sea more and more often until it finally rescinds all the wishes it has granted so far and the fisherman and his wife are returned to the ditch they were living in at the start of the story. I have always found this a compelling and disturbing story. How will I know when I have asked for too much? I might be getting close.

'Exit, pursued'
From Virgil, *The Aeneid*, chapter one, 'A Fateful Haven', lines 313–388: In the middle of a forest, Aeneas's mother crosses his path, but asks him questions as if he were a stranger. Nor does he recognise her, though he observes 'Your look's not mortal.' He asks her 'on what shore of the world are we cast up', and complains to her of the storms he has endured, how 'unknown and unprovisioned' he finds himself, till Venus 'chose to hear no more complaints / and broke in, midway through his bitterness'. This story of a son not recognising his mother, his mother refusing to hear his complaints, was very resonant to me. My translation of Venus as Love is not very satisfactory, since Love is not a name, but I do not think Venus in translation equals Love the way it would need to for it to be retained.

'My brother, twelve swans'
The story of the sister who has to knit twelve garments for twelve brothers, to turn them back from swans to men, has been told in many versions. Twelve swans make an appearance in *The Aeneid*, also, straight after the passage referred to above; in lines 391–402 Venus tells Aeneas that twelve swans have flown down from the sky, and that he should read this as a good omen, a sign that his ships have come in. Soon after this, he recognises her as his mother, but by then she has departed.